Leadership:

Essential Skills to Motivate and Influence People Around You

Table of Contents

Introduction

I want to thank you and congratulate you for purchasing the book, "**Leadership: *Essential skills to motivate and influence people around you – Maximize your leadership potential***".

This book contains proven steps and strategies on how to awaken, utilize, and maximize the natural leadership potential that you possess.

Leadership opportunities are not just confined in the workplace. Each day, in common life situations, a couple of leadership opportunities actually present themselves to you. To be a leader is to be responsible for your domain, whether that is the office, your team, your business, your field of study, your home, or your neighborhood. Contrary to what most people believe, leadership doesn't come from a position, a title, or even a crown. It is not who you are that makes you a leader. It's what you do, and more importantly, it's how you do it. Each time you make a decision about your life, you practice leadership. You actually become a leader each time you influence someone towards a certain path. Through this book, you will learn the true definition of leadership, the common misconceptions, and the most valuable qualities of a true leader.

The ancient model of command and control leadership is growing less and less applicable in modern work environments. The current trend is knocking down organizational structure. It's a great thing that people are starting to look for more than just a satisfactory job. Smart individuals are searching for careers that enable them to become more actively involved in decision-making. Whether you're a business owner, a manager, or an employee aspiring for a leadership role, this book will teach you strategies on how to motivate others, to increase your level of influence, and to nurture your innate leadership potentials.

Thanks again for downloading this book, I hope you enjoy it!

Chapter 1: Understanding Leadership

What is Leadership?

Leadership, in the simplest sense, refers to a process of social influence which involves maximizing the efforts and the potentials of other people in order to achieve certain goals.

Note the important elements of this definition:

Social Influence means that the source of leadership is neither power nor authority. Hence, it is possible for you to be the owner of a company and yet fail to be a leader.

Other people are important for leadership to occur.

The inclusion of a *Goal* means that in order for one's influence to be called leadership, there has to be an intended outcome.

What are the common misconceptions about leadership?

Leadership does not stem from seniority or from one's position in any hierarchy. Senior executives are senior executives, but that doesn't necessarily mean that they're leaders. Leadership does not equate to management either. A manager is a manager. A good manager is a good manager. Still, that doesn't automatically make him a leader. In the end, managers manage. Leaders lead. It's that simple.

Leadership doesn't have anything to do with titles. Even the person who earns the smallest salary in the company has the potential to be a leader. Leadership is dynamic, meaning it continuously moves throughout the system depending on the current priority. No single individual has ultimate control over it. As such, all members of your team may have the opportunity to handle a leadership role at some point.

Leadership does not come from personal characteristics either. Contrary to what most people believe, there's no such thing as a "born leader". The truth is all of us possess the potential to be powerful leaders. Just because a person is dominant, authoritarian, or charismatic, it doesn't necessarily make him a leader. Furthermore, leadership does not follow a particular style. Thus, you can work behind the curtain and still be a leader.

Contrary to what you might frequently see in the movies, the great leader is not a "lone wolf"; a person who isolates himself from the pack or the "superman" who does everything himself/herself to save the day. This concept of leadership might've been applicable during the time of hunters and gatherers where the strongest survive, but times have changed and we're now way beyond this kind of basic biological functioning. The truth is if you want to be the alpha, then you need others to back you.

While it's necessary for a leader to possess a certain degree of expertise in his field or his business, he doesn't have to know the answers to everything. Leadership is all about collaboration. It's all about including and motivating others to create solutions. A true leader must be a good problem-solver, but more important than that is that he must have curiosity and know how to ask all the right questions so that he can work together with the members of his team to arrive at the best solutions. Ultimately, leadership is not about people. It is about results.

Lastly, leadership is never about succeeding all the time. You don't have to have a perfect record to be a leader. In fact, failure is necessary because it gives way to improvement and innovation. True leaders are not afraid of dreaming and exploring. They understand that they need such courage to inspire their followers to dream and to explore. True leaders are not afraid of evolution.

Chapter 2: How to be a True Leader

So what does it take to be a leader?

To be a leader, you first need to believe that all people are valuable. Each person has his own strengths whether he realizes it or not. To be a leader means looking for and spotting that potential in each of your followers. Then, you cultivate that potential and discover how you can use it to meet your goals.

Ultimately, to be a leader, you have to possess the power to maximize potential within yourself, within any situation, and within others. Leadership is all about awakening and nurturing leadership within your employees or your followers. It's all about helping every member of your team become leaders in their own right.

What are the qualities of a true leader?

A true leader has a vision.

To *lead* means to direct to a certain course. Hence, a leader needs to have a direction. Or more specifically, he has to have a vision. He needs to know exactly where he wants to be just as his followers need to know where he is taking them. Moreover, a leader has to know how to communicate that goal to others. He makes an effort so that others will see his vision just as he sees it. A leader motivates others so that his goal also becomes their goal.

A true leader is honest.

When a team of people becomes your responsibility, then it is all the more important for you to possess honesty and transparency. Remember that your business and everyone working under you and with you are a reflection of yourself. Make integrity the foundation of your business and your company so your team will follow you by example. Whatever image that your brand or business is promoting, you need to live up to that standard. Your team needs to live up to that standard as well.

A true leader understands the value of delegation.

Leadership is not just your business. It's everyone's business. That is, everyone on your team. Part of being a leader is organizing and prioritizing. False leaders feel threatened by the idea of sharing their power, but in reality, assigning tasks and authorizing capable members of your team to make certain decisions will prevent you from stretching yourself thin. By having more time in your hands, you can focus on high-priority tasks and pursue bigger goals.

Figure out which tasks are best suited for each of your team members based on their individual strengths. Determine which responsibilities team members are most passionate about and have the opportunity to grow and then place them there. They are more likely to yield better results if they love what they're doing. Unless you can trust your team to work towards your vision, you will have neither the time nor the energy to take your brand or your business to the next level.

A true leader recognizes the importance of effective communication.

Your vision may seem perfect, but that may only be in your head. It is important to have a clear goal in mind, but it is just as important to be able to explain that goal to your team. In the end, you must ensure that you are all on the same page and that you are all putting your combined time and efforts towards the same vision.

Ask yourself these questions:

When I speak, do I believe what I'm saying?

Are my words congruent with my actions?

Do others feel safe about talking to me?

Great leaders do not only possess good speaking skills, they are also good listeners. Listen actively to your team's concerns. Do not just pay attention to what they're saying, but also take note of how they're saying it. Genuinely care about their opinions and seek their response. More than being communicative, you also need to be collaborative. Encourage your team members to voice out their ideas and give reward and recognition where they are due.

As a leader, you need to establish clear communication lines. Establish a clear chain of command. Who should your team members go to first if there are any concerns? Do you think that an open door policy will work best for your workplace? Is there a need for you to converse with your employees on a daily basis? Do you need to meet with each other at the end of the week? It is important that you make yourself available to discussing issues within the workplace.

A true leader is optimistic.

Low morale results to low production. Effective communication is also vital in boosting the team's morale when faced with challenges. What if your website crashes? What if your funds are depleted? What if you lose a valuable client? During these moments, you should be able to control damage within the workplace and to maintain the positive atmosphere conducive for creativity and productivity.

Ex:

Crack a few appropriate jokes to lessen the tension in a situation.

Meet with the team and discuss the lessons behind the struggles.

Encourage employees to plan their weekend trips.

Offer free-flowing coffee for your workers.

Celebrate small successes. If your company has reached a milestone (ex. 1,000 followers on Facebook, then congratulate everyone and pass out chocolates!)

It's small things like these that will save your team from burnout.

A true leader is confident.

A true leader remains confident even at times when his business is in trouble. Even at times when things don't go as planned. This will prevent panic and keep the team focused on their tasks and on the bigger picture. Teach others, by example, to always look ahead and move forward.

Do not mistake confidence in leadership with arrogance. After all, humility is also a virtue that leaders must possess. A true leader knows when to accept his mistakes and how to apologize for them when needed.

A true leader is intuitive. What would you do if you find yourself in unchartered territory? This is when you learn to trust your gut. Thus, in order to be a good leader, you need to be able to trust yourself. It also takes a great deal of courage to admit that you don't know or understand something. A confident leader seeks help when needed. While a true leader is aware of his own strengths, he also knows that his team members possess complementary strengths that can help make up for his weak areas.

A true leader displays commitment.

It's not just about being committed by heart. It's about commitment through action. It's all about practicing what you preach.

Commitment to a solo athlete means getting back into the field after an injury. When you're a leader the same thing is true except the responsibility is greater because you're working with a team and you're not just responsible for yourself, but also for others as well.

Instill a sense of pride in your team by working hard and turning up quality results. Be a man/woman of your word and fulfill your obligations and your promises. If you promised to discuss an issue with an employee, make time for it. An unfulfilled expectation may be the death of your credibility and character

Be punctual at meetings even when you know that others are willing to wait for you. This will show your subordinates that you value their time. This will show them that their time has value, that *they* have value.

Ex:

Napoleon Bonaparte worked side by side with his men, fighting in the battles and even performing tasks assigned to the lowest ranking soldier. This, in turn, boosted the men's morale and increased their devotion to him.

Ask yourself these questions:

How do I choose to spend my time?

Did I do my best today?

A true leader is creative.

You need to understand that not all situations will call for a clear-cut decision. There are times when you need to use your creativity and be flexible enough to deviate from your plan. A great leader is skilled at thinking outside the box and making quick *and* sound decisions while under pressure. A greater leader would know when it's time to look to the team for assistance. To be a leader, you need to be able to accept the possibility that your subordinates may know more about something than you do. You need to see this as a great opportunity instead of a threat or a reflection of your weakness.

A true leader is competent.

Being means that you are able to say something, plan something, and do something in such a manner that it is clear to others that you know exactly what you're doing. It is because of this that they will want to follow you.

To be competent, you need to possess an aura of readiness. You mustn't be afraid of challenges and of the idea of improvement.

Ex:

When your superior increases your responsibilities, don't think of it as extra burden. Instead, think of it as extra trust and be proud of it.

When faced with an unfamiliar task, fight your fear. Approach the new task with curiosity and optimism.

Chapter 3: Leadership and Motivation

How do I motivate others and maximize their potentials?

One thing that you need to understand about motivation is that it goes deeper than the incentive at the end. The incentive increases enthusiasm towards work that will inevitably lead to accomplishing the goal. On the other hand, motivation makes the person want to work because he wants to achieve the goal, because there is something in it for him. Motivation, in the simplest sense, refers to the reason behind a person's actions.

A motivated individual is ultimately more productive than an incentivized individual because he will push himself harder than any boss ever could. He will yield great results and do the right things even when no one is watching.

The first step is to listen.

Some have this misguided belief that motivation begins with a powerful speech. Before you say anything, listen to others first. What are their needs? What do they want? Next, ask yourself: *How can I use those needs and wants to make them do what I need them to do?* It's all about tying up other people's wants and needs with your ultimate goal.

Another skill you must possess is to vocalize others' wants and needs for them. Some people cannot verbalize what they want, but if you develop the words to speak it out loud for them, they will look up to you as their advocate. It's about making your team feel that you're on their side.

Ask all the right questions.

The right questions are open-ended and encourage exchange.

Ex:

"What excites you about this job?"

"What is that one thing that you've always wanted to do in your life?"

"What is success to you?"

Help your team see meaning in their work.

No matter how small a team member's role is, you need to make him realize that his contribution is important. A bricklayer may see his work as just that: stacking bricks. An incentivized bricklayer will stack bricks with more energy because he knows there's a reward if he meets the deadline. On the other hand, a motivated bricklayer will see his work as more than just stacking bricks. He sees himself laying the foundations of a great institution. He knows that this institution will make a difference to the world through its services and it becomes a source of pride for him to play a part in that. He will perform his duties well because he knows that what he's doing is important. Add to that his personal motivations (ex. providing for his family)

Let your team do their thing.

Avoid micromanaging. There is such a thing as being *too* helpful. When your team members feel like you're breathing down their necks, this is more likely to rattle them. Worse, they'll feel as if you don't trust them. So cut your team members some slack. As long as they are able to do what is needed of them, don't obsess over the small things.

Encourage others.

Don't just go about delegating tasks. Motivate your team members by making them understand why you've chosen to assign those tasks to them.

Ex:

"I noticed that you are really good in dealing with people and I believe that you'll be able to utilize and cultivate your skills if you work in the front desk."

Not the team leader? Encourage coworkers by giving genuine compliments like: "You are so good with people. I think you'll be great at the front desk."

Celebrate your team's accomplishments by "bragging" about it to your superiors. Just be sure you place the spotlight on your team members and not yourself.

Inspire your team to dream and to think big. Encourage them to create a positive vision of themselves several years from now.

Respect others.

Yelling, shaming, and making denigrating or sarcastic remarks towards your team members are a definite no. This creates a work environment where the team members will only do enough so as not to get yelled at by you. The rule is to treat the team the way you'd want them to treat your potential clients.

Chapter 4: Leadership and Influence

How do I increase my influence without relying on position?

Leadership is not about position. Rather, it is about action. Influence refers to your capacity to have an effect on someone's character, progress, or behavior. Whatever your position is in the workplace or in the community, building influence necessitates meticulous groundwork.

Understand your worth.

What are your skills? What are your strengths? Why should people want you to influence them? Whatever your job title is, it comes with a limited degree of influence. But rather than thinking of that as a limit, consider it as your starting point.

Earn others' trust.

It begins with building a good reputation for yourself. How did you choose to live your life over the past several years? You need to maintain consistency in all areas from your job performance to your character.

You can't be all sunshine one day and then be a grouch the next. People trust in stability. By submitting projects on time and producing consistently good results, people will come to think of you as someone whom they can rely on.

Determine what your values are and stick to them. If you are to influence others, you must not waver under pressure. When they see how calm and capable you can be during such circumstances, they will begin turning to you for guidance. It's for this reason why you must also look for a company whose values are in line with yours. To keep an unblemished reputation, you should refrain from being too involved and making too many promises.

Establish a good relationship with others.

First impressions do last, so mind your appearance. Know that there is a great difference between dressing to impress and *dressing to influence*. Dressing to impress means donning your best garments and strutting your stuff so others notice you and admire you. On the other hand, dressing to influence requires you to ask this question: *What would a leader look like to this/these person/s?* Is this group's perception of a leader someone who wears expensive designer suits? Or would this team be more comfortable following orders from someone who looks and dresses just like them?

People instinctively look for faces in the crowd that resemble theirs. Likewise, they tend to trust people who remind them of themselves quite easily. Upon connection, immediately be alert for any common ground. This is where your observation skills and active listening skills will become valuable in picking up cues. Single out any similarities that you have with the person and work from there. At times, it is useful to match and mirror other people's behaviors including their mannerisms, patterns of speech, and level of energy.

Focus on others instead of yourself.

People have this natural need to be liked and accepted. Feed this need and you gain instant influence. Get to know as much as you can about your coworkers. Instead of waxing poetically about your stellar past achievements, shine the spotlight on their achievements. What makes you proud about this group? What is the group's greatest accomplishment over the past year?

Remember names. Remember things. Remember how your team member mentioned last week that her mom was in the hospital. Inquire about her mother's wellbeing. She'll be surprised and pleased that you remembered. Bring up how tidy your employee's work desk is. He'll be surprised and pleased that you noticed. Call people by their names. People tend to respond to favors positively when you address them with their names. Also, politeness goes a long way. A simple "thank you", or "I appreciate it" will encourage people to respond more positively to your requests.

Use emotional connection to forge a bond between yourself and others.

Stimulate the pleasure-reward part of their brain so they will feel warm around you. One thing that you need to know about charisma is that it's not about you. It's about *them*. It's about how you make people feel when they're with you. When you make people feel positive about themselves then they will naturally keep wanting to be around you, to talk to you, to listen to you, and to be influenced by you.

Use proper body language.

An influential body language depends entirely on the situation. A power body language consists of the head held high, arms loose, chest out, and shoulders set back. Maintain this winning posture even in times of crisis and others will look to you for strength.

If you need to show someone that you are engrossed in what he's saying, lean over and make sure that you point your feet towards him. Likewise, you need to learn other people's body language and nonverbal cues so you may gauge the proper time to drop a suggestion.

Ex: When you notice that the person's eyes are dilated, this means he's interested and it may be the opportune moment to sell your idea.

If you want others to approach you, refrain from assuming a closed body posture (ex. crossed arms or legs, bag sitting on your lap) Maintain eye contact and commence your speech with a smile.

Nodding is contagious. Speakers tend to nod their heads to get their audiences to nod back in agreement.

If you want to appear important then try taking up as much space as you can. Lean back with your legs open and use broad gestures.

Ask for favors. Give favors.

When you ask people for favors, you are playing to their ego. It shows that you believe in their expertise.

Be kind to everyone. You'll never know when you'll be needing their support. Another strategy that you can employ is planting tiny seeds of favors here and there and then reaping the rewards later. It's in people's nature to give back for fear of being called freeloaders. An example of using this technique is when companies hand out freebies to potential clients during a product demonstration whether or not they purchase anything. About half of those people who received freebies will be influenced to buy the product because it is deeply rooted in our brain that if we take something, we have to give something in return.

Rub elbows with the right people.

Learn from top influencers in your field. Study their strategies and their approach. Ask them to be your mentors. Be friends with them if you can. A great influencer knows the value of having the right connections. As previously mentioned, an important part of leadership is accepting that all people have value. This person may not be able to do anything for you right now but he can connect you with someone who can help you in your goals. So broaden your circles. Acquaint yourself with people from various walks of life. You may not be the boss in your company but if you know the right people outside the company (ex. potential clients and suppliers) then you can become a valuable asset.

Make yourself indispensable to others.

Naturally, you need to possess knowledge and skill in your field. But another trait you must possess is the ability to teach others to be self-reliant so as to provide them with a sense of pride. Don't be afraid that by teaching your team to develop their own skills, you'll end up being useless to them. The truth is if you're able to make people feel proud of themselves, they'll always run to you for guidance and approval. More importantly, they'll always remember you as the source of that positive emotion. They'll keep gravitating towards you.

Another way of making yourself indispensable is developing ability to resolve conflicts and to facilitate people to work together and set aside their differences for the common goal.

Remember that people tend to forget what you look like and what you did but if there's one thing that will stick with them, it's how you made them feel.

You don't necessarily have to know everything. You just need to know who's good at which tasks. As previously mentioned, you mustn't limit yourself to your department.

Ex: Who's the best person to approach in the IT department?

Who's the most skilled person in graphics?

By knowing all these things, you'll be able to direct others to the right people, thus strengthening your status as the ultimate go-to person.

If you're not in a leadership position just yet, you should mentor a co-worker who is having difficulty with his work. This is the best way to practice. One person will perceive you as a leader and that's a good start.

Seek continuous self-improvement by taking classes and attending seminars to polish your present skills, learn new ones, and keep up with the trend.

Chapter 5: Nurturing Your Innate Leadership Potentials

Develop your leadership style.

Developing a leadership style is easier once you've identified and developed your strengths. You find out what you're good at and then you play to that strength.

To determine your strengths, try this activity:

At the end of the week, make a list of five things that worked well in your career, your life, etc. Do the same the following week.

The next thing you must do is to identify your weaknesses.

List down: What are the things that went wrong this week?

What are the things I could've done to make it better?

Change your mindset. Step outside your comfort zone by trying unfamiliar activities such as a new sport or a new hobby. Consider this as a baby step to taking on a leadership style that you're not used to. If you think you need to be a more aggressive leader, then try a contact sport. If you're having difficulty in taking risks, then learn a risky sport. If you think you need to be more relaxed as a leader then explore relaxing activities like pottery.

Develop your strengths.

Defeat automatic negative thoughts about yourself by using logic.

Ex:

"I can't be a leader. I'm too shy."

Logic: "Being an introvert doesn't mean that I'm not leader material. I'm good at what I do. I don't have to be a social butterfly to share my skills with the team."

Make a journal that contains your achievements in the past and revisit it each time your self-esteem could use a boost.

The worst thing you can do is to depend on others (your boss, your coworkers, your community) for acceptance and fulfillment. Learn to discover fulfillment on your own.

Write down all the things you love about your current job. Why are you proud about it? Do you believe that you're doing something worthwhile?

Harboring resentment will prevent you from becoming a leader. Don't dwell on your failures. Stop thinking about opportunities which are overdue or whatever it is that you believe are owed to you. Instead, concentrate on continuously improving yourself and find ways to stand out. Improve your performance. Give extra time and effort and perform small tasks with love. Even when no one notices it, learn to experience satisfaction in a job well done.

Incorporate these positive affirmations in your daily routine:

I am a natural leader.

I am punctual. I am responsible. I am productive.

Others follow me because I am trustworthy, competent, and reliable.

Develop your communication skills as a leader.

Consider this stressful and frustrating situation: You're struggling to get your message across in a meeting. Your colleges are opposing you. They're questioning your proposal, doubting your ability to make decisions. You try to explain, try to make them realize your vision but your brain is flooded with cortisol. Your advanced thought processes shuts off and thus you lose your ability for strategy and empathy and trust. Instead, your brain immediately goes into the default responses: fight (you keep arguing non-productively) or flight (you just choose to let the group have their way).

Let's say you win an argument. Your brain is flooded with adrenaline. Yes you win! But the danger here is that this feel-good hormone will keep you craving for more. Hence, you keep fighting. Because you feel like proving one point is not enough. Unfortunately, such a behavior can cause a great deal of irreparable damage to your professional relationships.

So how do true leaders communicate?

True leaders create rules of engagement. They don't just storm off to a meeting. Prior to the conference, they prepare themselves for every possibility so as to prevent themselves from being tripped by tricky patterns of conversation.

True leaders know how to lend an empathic ear. They talk less and then they listen more. When you do this, others have a tendency to return the favor. When it's your turn to speak, they'll give you the same respect and attention that you've given them.

True leaders give everyone an opportunity to speak. Some individuals have a tendency to dominate the conversation. A leader will make a plan beforehand so that all members of the team will be able to provide input. The leader collaborates with the team to find out who has expertise in which topics and then opens the floor to various speakers.

When you do these, instead of experiencing a surge in cortisol or adrenaline levels, your oxytocin level will increase. This hormone is triggered by human connection. In turn, it activates networks in your prefrontal cortex so as to nurture emotions of trust and open communication.

Develop your problem solving skills.

Leaders understand that the primary phase of problem solving is the part which requires the most analysis. Some are too eager to jump into possible solutions without analyzing if the problem really is a problem at all. Identify the nature of the problem. Is it composed of several small problems which you need to address one by one? If yes, which of these problems should you address first? If you solve one of the smaller problems, would it automatically get rid of the rest?

> Develop your decision-making skills.

When making decisions, you should strive to find the balance between intuition and reason. Begin with reason. Collect the facts. Then, after you've come up with a tentative decision, consider your intuition. Does this decision feel right? If it doesn't, why not?

You need to ensure that whatever decisions that you make, they will be carefully and promptly implemented. Furthermore, when making a decision that will affect the entire team, you need to know how to express to the members the benefits of that decision.

Understand that not everything is an "either-or" problem. Not everything is answerable by yes or no. Instead of asking: "Should we purchase a new company car?", try this approach: "Let's decide on the best mode of transportation for our employees."

Conclusion

Thank you again for downloading this book!

I hope this book was able to help you to understand the basics of leadership, what it means to be a leader, and how to develop your skills as a leader.

The next step is to apply these steps and strategies to motivate like-minded individuals so that together, you can turn your common vision into reality.

Finally, if you enjoyed this book, then I'd like to ask you for a favor, would you be kind enough to leave a review for this book on Amazon? It'd be greatly appreciated!

Thank you and good luck!

www.ingramcontent.com/pod-product-compliance
Lightning Source LLC
Chambersburg PA
CBHW070522210526
45169CB00027B/1387